*Sounds from the Beach Vendor's
Coins Mixed with the Seagulls'
Huah Huah Huah*

Sounds from the Beach Vendor's Coins Mixed with the Seagulls' Huah Huah Huah

Growing up Brooklyn

Dian Cunningham Parrotta

RESOURCE *Publications* • Eugene, Oregon

SOUNDS FROM THE BEACH VENDOR'S COINS MIXED WITH THE
SEAGULLS' HUAH HUAH HUAH
Growing up Brooklyn

Copyright © 2020 Dian Cunningham Parrotta. All rights reserved. Except for brief quotations in critical publications or reviews, no part of this book may be reproduced in any manner without prior written permission from the publisher. Write: Permissions, Wipf and Stock Publishers, 199 W. 8th Ave., Suite 3, Eugene, OR 97401.

Resource Publications
An Imprint of Wipf and Stock Publishers
199 W. 8th Ave., Suite 3
Eugene, OR 97401

www.wipfandstock.com

PAPERBACK ISBN: 978-1-7252-5642-2
HARDCOVER ISBN: 978-1-7252-5643-9
EBOOK ISBN: 978-1-7252-5644-6

Manufactured in the U.S.A.   DECEMBER 17, 2019

Dedicated to my large extended family who inspired it but are no longer here to read it.

Contents

Acknowledgments | ix
Introduction | xi

just playing garbage men: 1960's trash pickup | 1
all on hot concrete and asphalt streets | 2
Work from home | 4
Ken, lock your car doors | 5
gots teaching the kids racism | 8
at the cost of that weapon of surprise | 12
doodie on her swing | 13
the relatives in Bay Ridge, Brooklyn | 14
Where real important things are happening | 15
60s grammar school days | 17
Oh, irrevocable | 18
the electrical shock | 19
that Staten Island ferry ride in the early 60s | 20
but daddy can't read | 21
discovering patterns and poetry | 23
my Lancelot | 24
too hot to sleep | 26
the beehive hairdo | 27
but my mommy says | 28
It's daddy's nighttime | 29
Myrtle the box turtle | 30
remembering that dead art of tv repair | 31
From Flatbush, with love | 32

An Irish Gavotte Dance to the Catskills from Flatbush | 34

The Woodstock Campers behind My Grandpa's the Sullivan House | 36

The banging of pots, pot covers, metal spoons on pans | 37

my father's face | 38

from a lighted meteoroid shooting around in outer space | 39

a heavy upon the world | 41

anthropomorphizing | 42

An ode to Trader Joe's Flowers | 44

scrap paper on Ars Poetica | 45

Ode to the Ginkgo Biloba tree and to her leaves | 46

my mom moves in with me after when dad passes | 47

Acknowledgements

ACKNOWLEDGEMENTS TO MY FAVORITE Langston Hughes, Pablo Neruda, Gwendolyn Brooks, Emily Dickinson, Walt Whitman, Robert Frost and my dearest Sandra Cisneros, whose writings has helped me reach many thousands of young teens in my English courses. I love teaching *House on Mango Street* with the kids and that short story, "*Eleven*" has always been a big hit in class too.

Dedicated to Professor Beth Mead, the director of Lindenwood's MFA Program. Thank you so much Professor Gillian Parrish.

Great thanks to the major professor overseeing my thesis project, Professor Eve Jones.

Thank you, Professor D'Souza, Professor Pryor, Professor Candice, Professor Hollingsworth and to Professor Vickers whose guidance and encouragement was invaluable.

Thank you to my fellow classmates for the inspiration you gave me through our writing experiences and discussions. You all inspire me.

Thank you, Lindenwood University's MFA Program. You will all always be a part of me in some way.

Introduction

THE BEACH VENDOR'S COINS Mixed with the Seagulls' Huah Huah Huah—is an autobiographical poetry chapter book. The poems focus on an impoverished but hopeful young girl and her large extended family living in Flatbush, Brooklyn, New York City, during the civil right movement, 1960-1980. A chapter book of poems about the wonderful and sometimes not so wonderful memories from the past. A collection of poems on childhood that will make you nostalgic if you are a baby boomer but if not, these childhood poems might bring a new perspective on how different life growing up today is than it was when the writer was growing up.

In the Brooklyn borough you soon enough recognize which areas you are in kinship with. The cultural divisions in Brooklyn were strictly observed. Yet at the same time people would break the boundaries and find themselves in a new cultural zone where language, foods, and activities were different but the one thing everyone had in common was that all kids, no matter what race or religion could pretty much come and go at will. There were no boundaries there. The only rule all the kids seem to have followed without ever breaking is to be home when they saw the lighting bugs.

Introduction

It's Brooklyn, 1960, in the Flatbush neighborhood where the Italians, Irish, German and Jewish people lived and yes at that time segregation and racism were unfortunately still persevering with many movements going on heading towards the right direction. The young girl in the photograph above, just standing right behind her little sister, Karen, is me when I lived in a duplex shared by my two families who used to live all in one big house, on Parkville Avenue, just down the street from a great Tudor Gothic church building named St. Rose of Lima Catholic Church but had to move due to the city needing the property to build an apartment building in its place. The family had to move but could not find one house big enough to contain this large extended assembly, so the two families bought a duplex on New York Avenue.

Introduction

Grandma Tess, with her two high school aged daughters, Marylou and Paula moved into the upstairs duplex apartment and Frankie joined the army and Johnny got married. Then this young girl's dad, mom, one sister and one brother (eight more years after another brother would be born) lived in the downstairs apartment and don't worry you will meet them all presently living inside my poetry. Come meet my family.

It's Brooklyn, 1960, in the Flatbush section of Brooklyn and not too far away from Coney Island and all you need to know about Coney Island as George C. Tilyou, builder of Coney Island's Steeplechase Park says, "If Paris is France, Coney Island, between June and September, is the world." And yes, this girl's family would all pile into the family station wagon on some summer evenings to head off to Nathan's Coney Island restaurant for hot dogs and orders of crinkle-cut French fries served in a paper bag for all to share. And the two miles of beaches and boardwalk of slanted wooden planks offered the working class a cheap escape like each being on there own run-away carousal horse let loose into the amazing thrills of Brooklyn's Riviera, Coney Island.

A favorite writer of mine is Sandra Cisneros, who talks about birthdays in her short story, *Eleven,* and she explains "they don't understand about birthdays and what they never tell you is that when you're eleven, you're also ten, and nine, and eight, and seven, and six, and five, and four, and three, and two and one." Sandra describes growing old "is like an onion or the rings inside of a tree trunk or like her little wooden dolls that fit one inside the other." So that being said *Growing Up Brooklyn,* where the speaker is often the kid inside of me is narrating.

So, let young Dian Cunningham take you from my Introduction to just spilling you right into of her story. Let's listen to this young girl in the picture narrate many of the following pages of vignettes and poetry in this brief poetry chapter book titled *The Beach Vendor's Coins Mixed with the Seagulls' Huah Huah Huah. Let her poetry and vignettes* show you what life was really like heard through this young voice chattering from her top bunk down to her sleeping sister this early morning back in Brooklyn on July 5, 1965 whisperin down to sleeping sister in a snore:

Introduction

I

Karen, there's a seagull wailing gull-bird noisy huahs on our sill sitting with its wings wapping and white

huah huah huah   huah huah huah   huah huah huah

Having deliberately slept in her clothes, just to be able to be the first one outside in the morning, ten-year-old Diane Cunningham is ready to go search for any stray firecrackers that were either dropped from a kid's pocket or ones that failed to detonate and had been simply called out as duds. During the mid-60s Brooklyn permitted the use of fireworks only on the evening of Independence Day and this made July 5th an unsanctioned holiday for any child that was willing to skip morning cartoons and scour the ground on hands and knees. She stops a moment and stares at Karen's sleeping fat face. Then she reaches for the plastic Jack-O-Lantern that she stashed away under her bedroom desk.

This pumpkin should hold hundreds and hundreds, she thinks as her static strands of hair flies straight to the orange plastic container making Diane almost look like a just lit fire-spitting firecracker and tries to touch the seagull on the sill, but he flies away   huah huah huah

"I say comrade Jack-O-Lantern, let's go wake up Kenny," whispers Diane tip toes out of her bedroom banging the plastic pumpkin softly on the walls down the hallway and bobbing it on each dining room chair. The early morning sun shines brightly into Kenny's room only lighting up Diane's very disappointed face. "He has already gone out to hunt the streets for lost explosives without me," saying with tightened pinched up lips in a knot.

I can't believe he left already and without calling me. He woke up, went out and left the front door wide opened, Diane whines to herself but then remembers:

Introduction

My dad is getting a new car today.

Stepping out in front of her house and climbs right up the parking sign pole, and takes another look down the block, and then in the other directions, and notices the American flags flying at half-staff. Flags are flying from windowsills, balconies, and from stoops making any bystander feel proud to be an American. She sees the neighbors' barbecue grills still sitting out in the curb, from the block party the night before. The covered card tables were still out in front, dressed up in bright red, white and blue tablecloths; those cloths and all the flags were yelling out from the top of their lungs, "God, Oh God, Bless our sweet America."

The air is still; it smells of the firecracker finale, ash cans, cherry bombs that were blasted up the night before, mixed with some of the Italian neighbors' freshly fried Zeppole, that deep fried pastry dunked in powder sugar, everyone on the block loved. What can I say but that this is Brooklyn, New York.

Diane counts only four big kids down the block combing the China red and white and blue papered streets searching for any gun powder-filled crackers and notices that Louie Ventura and Dennis Buckley are not there. They were drafted and she knew that meant that if you are 18 years old you have to go fight a war in a place called Viet Nam. That you get to wear a really cool uniform with your hair buzzed off and get to knock on the neighbors' doors hugging them goodbye. And then thinks again: *My dad is getting a brand-new car today.*

Some of the girls run to get brooms to sweep the streets, making large piles of blown up paper, burned up metal sparklers, cigarette butts, empty match books in a colorful chunk mound right in front of Diane's house.

Introduction

"Ohhhhh. Nana, my dad is going to buy a new car today," whispering the good news to this German born white-haired lady. "God bless your family," Nana says. "*Vhat* an exciting time it must be for your family, my dear," says in a deep European accent.

"Girls, you are doing such a good job cleaning our street," Grandma Tessy yells out from her top floor den window.

Soon after this young crowd of kids form into two teams as Veronica Carter, tall the 12 year old with the very long bangs almost covering her eyes, who points and pokes each kid's shoulder, one by one, saying, "Eni Meeni Ib sa Deen nee, Ab Ab Bumble Leen ni, Atcha Catcha Om bla Atcha and OUT GOES Y… O… U…!"

The teams are chosen, and the soft rubber pink Spalding ball is out along with Marty Mintz's short green broom stick. A car passes slowly down the street with blasting Roger Miller's No phone, no pool, no pets / I ain't got no cigarettes/ Ah but, two hours of pushing broom/ Buys an eight by twelve four-bit room/ I'm a man of means, by no means/ King of the road

Kenny ignores the kids all singing King of the road and says, "This sewer cover will be home plate. First plate will be Giordano's car. Second is the fire hydrant.

At that moment, Mr. Cunningham is spotted by the children.

"Diane here comes your dad in his new car," they all yow out in a caw.

The children are quiet, and one points to the old green station wagon scraping down the street. One of the tires is almost flat and the car's tail pipe drags on the hot black asphalt. Mr. Cunningham, a red-haired Irishman with a bright happy smile, gets out of the car finding the children all looking at his car. Diane stands there squeezing the pink Spalding ball in her hands.

Introduction

"Hey, Diddles," he sings out, "I know it needs some fixing up, but this car will be able to take us to Saugerties, next week to visit Grandpa and Grandma GeeBee, for a ten-day-long vacation."

"Daddy, I thought you were going to buy a brand-new car."

Then little Kenny calls out, "Yeah, we are going to the Hudson River Valley again this year! Take the suitcases down from the attic!" He jumps up and down screaming out, "Yeah, I will bring my BB gun and shoot some plates in the woods. Yeah,   yeah   yeah   huah   huah huahhuah

"Dollie, this is new for us," the dad says in good spirits while watching Kenny as he marches around the street out of his happiness. Stamping his feet and saluting to the other kids, like a trained soldier who was just awarded a medal for just about any of his singularly meritorious actions.

Mr. Cunningham waves up to Grandma Tessy who is now hanging halfway out the second story window with her dark sunglasses on and with a smile.

"Congratulations," Grandma Tessy shouts out the window.

"Thanks, Mom," Mr. Cunningham smiles back and then runs up the stoop steps and calls for his wife to come and take a look at his new car, while the kids decide to go play School in Terry McKiernan's garage, and within seconds, disappear down the street. The seagulls' squawking chirp screech and caw Huahhuahhuah   Coney Island Beach   huah huah huah at ten   huah huahhuah

II

Diane sits on the curbside pretending to be looking in the pile of swept up debris for some more lost July 4th fireworks; her straggly long hair and

Introduction

bangs covering her tears and squatted up body looking like a tree stump dumped brink. But now like magic, the barefooted Tom Boy remembers they're going to Getcha Hot Knishes beach at ten and looks up and waves up to Grandma Tessy whose looking like a Pileated Pecker peering out her den with dark sunglasses on yelling, "We're going to Coney Island Beach at ten." as if a strong sea breeze and the seagulls' huah-ings blew her up to the two stilt sticks gracefully wading too slowly down the block towards M. Then almost halfway down, and to her left, she squawks-yawps-caterwauls a long-mumbled wail to Mrs. Hasselman, who is usually seen sitting there in her alleyway chair under her oak tree's sunshade and sun leaves.

"Mrs. Hasselman. **"I'm going to the Coney Island at ten."**

Diane struggles stamping about in one place on stilts. She moves one leg lath and holds the other slat at still. "How do you like how I can stand on stilts?" not knowing, Mrs. Hasselman can't see cause she's blind but says, "You're a maneuvering shorebird placating it's time with the fish. I'm thinking you're a Banded Stilt legged bird,"

"I'm not sure what I look like, but I can't stand still on stilts in one spot, Mrs. Hasselman I gotta head back to pack. We're leaving at ten to go to the beach."

And Mrs. Hasselman heard the wooden boards **WHACH WHACK**

and "*dip dip dip*," of her feet slap the cemented slabs on hot sidewalk. the "*dip, dip, dip*," she gyrates backwards in a spin down the street to her right, towards home, snaps up and down, trying not to step on the sidewalk cracks. "Step on a crack, break your mother's back. Step ona..." Her song singing bringing cheer to Mrs. Hasselman as she's thinking *she's just like blooms from a hellebore* and arches her back, into a luxurious stretch, just as an old tabby cat.

III

Getchya hot square potato knishes, hot dogs here, eking out a living that unlicensed vendor's honest hustle's old script-sales-bait pitches across the grandest Dreamland Park he knows and the Steeplechase and Lunar Parks too and along the *under the board walk zone, the People's Playground*

Introduction

peddling below the rumbling thunderous roars of the armies of coaster rides & Scream Zone with Big Mamma Cyclone and the iconic memories of that wooden Switchback Railway that gravity pulled coaster's ghostly shrieks in the winding-up Victrola carny music sounds Julius Fucik's "*Entrance of the Gladiators*" and big band foxtrots' "*Fly Me to the Moon's*" 4/4 time beat long movements, like lovers, continuously falling, steps into stories, swings the Italian dark-skinned guy, goateed 40-something in mirrored aviator sunglasses with muscular tattooed forearms, the Coney Island Beach Vendor, in fly fishing gloves, dragging brown paper Gimbles-bags by and skirting around glorious bikinis sets on the two-piece beach of sun worshippers burrowing on top of beach blankets like oiled squirming fish waddle. Shirking and hollering out, *Getchya hot square potato knishes. Hot, Getchya hot dogs. Hot knishes here.* Arduous barefootsying round towels, boom boxes balancing on top of bags, the thermoses, umbrellas and sand chairs, like tracing crossword puzzles in sand or crisscrossing borders and boundaries navigating the narrows of nations. *Hot potato knishes, gettem here. Getchya hot dogs. Hot knishes.*

A tall that big blonde, in that glitziest swimsuit, dragging, a lug, that ice chesting through, grooming smooth snow board trails, burying more cigarette butts than seashells there. Tanned, huge-bouncing boobs hanging big with a Marylyn-Monroe-singing-softly-voice, crooning chiseled short sexy trills of *ice-cold orange creamsicles, popsicles, fudgsicles. Gotcha ice cold red, white and blue Rocket ice Pumps Pops. Iced cold cans of coke, root beer, orange sodas. And* gotta Killem, these Ballantine beers *blasts and gots* cigarettes. *Save me, one unsold cold one for Jimmy Gargiulo's my man.* The two wearing yellow-taxi-man Nickel-Plated Steel Money Changers with penny, nickel, dime and quarter barrels, swingin loosely on waistbands, round their bare bellies. Refracting splendid awe-inspiring masterpieces of stained-glass rainbows, scattering, like flying kaleido s c o p i c surfaces tilting against those heated wafting miscellaneous carnival Funnel Cakes, frying burgers, french fries, Coney's Cones whiffing out sugar smoke into a swelteringly against the beach's salty seawater smells. Aww, Coney Island, the buttress, a magical gem, a dreamland I used to know interwoven in the dithering washed out white noise of the vendors' coins mixing with seagulls'

huahhuahhuah huah huah huah huahhuahhuoh

just playing garbage men: 1960's trash pickup

Brooklyn garbage men wear the Mets or Yankees baseball caps and keep their mouths open while chewing gum. *Sorda* tilt your move and your jaw to the left and that's when ya grab the garbage can, let the falling trash-can-lid fall like this and didgeridoo the can down the cement paved alleyway. An easy roll-crash-bang, you know, those authentic street strains. Keep your shirt unbuttoned and your chest and belly sticking out and watchmedoingit. Don't forget to use those garden gloves when ya picking up the can and now the cans are real light because the garbage men just emptied them at noon. We can both be garbage men together and I think I have an extra piece of gum otherwise ya just gotta pretend you're chewing on it like how a Catskill cow chews grass. Keep ya mouth moving more. Oh, and, and swing your shoulders, a shove left then back, thrust right and forward. Push out your chest tossing the can if you can over your own stands or just up in the air and make a guttural clearing of the throat noise and spit like this. Then make those clanking aluminum-tins-banging garbage cans rattle-clack. The thrown-down-the-alleyway-metal-can receptacle bickers a sonorous resonant, a rich, full, booming metal-scratching-against-concrete scrape like a-long-full-throttle of a nasty, throated debate. Walk down to the next house and wave at my Grandma Tessy if she yells at you from the window from inside and say hi. Then walk down the street and pretend you are following the incredibly large white elephant, that loud-noisy-ass-truck working its way down past Mr. Liberman's and past the Ricciardi's and then past L up around K over towards Fresh Kills Landfills. You wanna whistle by twisting your tongue into a knot shelling out a long high shrill when you get there. Then yell. Cause we're acting like our Brooklyn's heroes like the cops and fire but garbage mans are oversized-colossals-bigs-leagues especially during those dog days cause the trash is smelly stinks and what's the word for how it smells after it rains? And then all the neighbors say, "Gud the garbage men came."

all on hot concrete and asphalt streets

S
t
   o
    o
     p
     b
       a
         l
            l
  5
    10
      20
        25

Fielder calls, "Ball's on Buckley's lawn."

Car passes down the street, makes the loose-sewer

-cover- manhole metal clank and clack.

Bicycles horns-trumpet

honking cars horns sound klaxon at the kids in the street, and the percussive

. . . honking cars horns sound klaxon at the kids in the street, and the percussive rings of bicycle bells tin ding- ding by, clinking small clicks that resonant a ring or a trilling dring or a tintinnabulous ding and bike handles' with pastel ribbons stream f L a P p I n g tha tha tha tha tha tha tha tha tha tha tha. bicycle spoke noisemaker sounds with baseball cards clipped on spokes

with clothes pins, motorcycle motor sounds, . . .

speeds by, and Grandma Tessy leans out the upstairs window with no screen and yells, "noooo nooooo OHHH noooooooooo" to the driver parking in front, "NOOOO parking in son-in-law's spot." and we all waves to grandma, an a seagull sounds out, an bike bells still ping.

"Ball broke two tulips," Fielder yells an a, "Mr. Gio's gots the ball again." Batter bunches up her fingers in her mouth and wet whistles a high pitch. Throws her new pensie pinkie at the stoop stairs

and spits.

"35 a high ball's 10. 45 nother high ball 55. that's nine innings, get the brooms. it's a sweep."

Work from home

Lenny, the Jewish jeweler

from the Mill Basin neighborhood

brought a giant jewelry clamp and a heavy iron roller machine down to my basement.

He gave my mom and the neighborhood ladies on my block a job, a-work-from-home-jewelry-making real job for cash and so they all worked in my basement sitting around card tables with fans on in a sweat shop with pliers and other tools to put together *Gogo belts* out of metal chain links with green plastic shapes, with rings and loops, with white leather squares and oversized geometric shapes like large circles, and oversized polka-dots, spirals, and hexagons and peace signs pendants and textured metals in atomic space -age shapes mod jewelry with groovy looks. Those Klinger sculptural stud clay polka dot mini hoop love knots with sticky back dots to make pretend you got pierced ears but don't have ear holes and those with flower shape statements while working and watching that old tv screen with the white dot disappearing closing down Star Trek on our broken basement TV screen that you can hear the sound but not see anything but random dot pixel pattern of static displayed on the set. I learned jewelry making terminology like it's blowing out- which means selling extremely well and minimalism and merchandizing, and what is promotional jewelry too. I learned what batches means like sets of earrings need to be put into the cardboard earring cards for jewelry displays, hang tags, with self-adhesive bags and tags often *pcs of 50* they would make and Aunt Mary Lou would say that Black ladies at her bank would say Shoooo-be-doo-da-day and she was saying Shooooo-be-doo-da-day a lot and I was too. New words were as wild as psychedelic tie dyes on the next each breath.

Ken, lock your car doors

Little Harlem in 1960s—where Haitian Black population boomed

It's not the July Fourth without that Dad's drive over to Bed-Stuy

for his yearly Firework-Package Pick Up to those row houses on Mac-Donough Street

from limestones to the modest brick and brownstone in ordered row-house to building tenements and flats buildings blocks and blocks

looking for Alopecia Dumont selling thrills

of the firework matts, cherry bombs, ash cans,

looking for the man not a hair on his head or eye lashes even

selling flags and unstamped North Carolina cigarettes and those fireworks those Brocks

Bombshell Repeaters, standard dizzle dazzle

bangs, screech owls and jumping jacks those

C.T. Brock & Cos Crystal Palace Gun powder Super

Dragons and sparklers down the alley ways

those behind the scene's secrets where the black girls wearing jequirity lady bug-beans jumping Double Dutch and laughing and me taking turning the rope in my brand new Beatlemania white go-go boots on with the Star-Spangled Banner on their Transistor radios and smelling the barbecue fires up for a block party later just like we're gonna have the black man with the white face is sitting on the stoop smiling calling my daddy, *my Cabby Red is here for the crackers*

And the kids are playing in water in gutters in street under opened fire hydrants sprays to sprinklers blastings the tenement kids in underclothes and trunks

The hot streets smelling like those Black Snakes Firework Pellets they selling all big 12 in a bag, grows into a massive flaming tower on the side in the street as they burn a watery steam fluffing up-base on fire and glowing, carbon dioxide gas burning on tar resurrecting black ash wiggling up and the Grandmas looking out windows and some outside in pretty Karabela dresses with

ruffles with ric rac serving bowls of peaches

with canned evaporated milk cream with fried

green sweet plantains and the little girls playing

whipping hand smacking into screeching louder those

clapping game songs with the same rhythm as of eenie

meanie sassaleeny right there under that Serpentine

weeping Cherry Tree twisting crawling branches diving back

down into the alley way ground with foliage with bright

green panicles with Caribbean archipelago planted intact to the sidewalks of colors smells teeming outdoor Kingston, Jamaica, Grenada to the sidewalks of New York that Haitian Creole heard then that Haitian lady and the Black American lady are fighting in the street and daddy says look away whispering *they don't like themselves* that other lady says ohhhh yes you are talking

to me so condescendingly with you reaching

for that American Dream

that ain't never there for you

Black just like me and yanking the woman's frills off her hand-Embroidery

from her fresh cotton Caribbean's pride

there with ruff and lace torn off

in the street black tar

heat and that red and blue torn fabrics getting wet floating

by the open fire hydrant

high-pressure sprays spurting skyward

under the jumping children those crafty tenement kids.

gots teaching the kids racism

We play *I Declare War* inside circles

drawn using pastel chalk sticks in the streets

throwing pink Spaldeens or Penzy Pinkies.

That Cold War is a hot issue yelling

I declare war on Russia and all Communists

With fears of nuclear annihilations

and we all throw our balls down on Russia and run.

And Sister Joseph Loretta tells us to hide-

cover-under-wooden-desks drills and prays

our nation is safe from that *Red Menace that Red Scare.*

Dr. Martin Luther is communist

and I love Lucy's Ricky Ricardo

is a communist and Langston Hughes and Charlie Chaplin too

and I only see black people at the zoo passing just through

the elephant and monkey houses them with lots of little girls with wild tiny braids

with colorful rubber bands and I smile and wave to them as you

grabbing my hand tightly pulling me into

a much safe closer. Our nation's homophobic

and blacks and gays are bad and Catholics

are too and I can't play with Debbie Landau's

friend Vivian who you say has the lips and that hair

but she sings Over the Rainbow sounding just as Judy Garland

sings so beautifully with moving hands

supporting unseen rhythms a storyteller singing

It's a Beautiful World she moves adding meaningful gestures

that portray sincere emotions to dreams we can't see yet.

My friend BeeBee, a Muslim Guyanaese,

 wasn't invited to my birthday party.

You say we don't have like those here inside our home.

Growing up Brooklyn reins anti-black caricatures

dark negativities portraying how lazy,

Ignorant, and obsessively self-indulgent noxious

racial slurs deliberately saying that N word, Spics, dirty wops, drunk Irish, cheap Jew people—

Puerto Ricans love killing cornered roaches, in pointed shoes so that's why they always wear

them and it aint's always easy seeing those with bad blows with no people's rights lefts and rights and all those can't come into our neighborhoods

or they be stealing our new bikes and not here on our blocks.

And I see those department store fights

hiding inside the racks of Easter clothes seeing that lady kicks

hard and remembering hearing it's like a plane flight landed

from Puerto Rico was full with Boricuases

come to our beaches just like you say cock

roaches from their day time hiding places

when the lights are out when all the white people

are leaving once the sun's going down and hearing salsa songs

and bomba music boom boom boxes are carrying tree-tie hammocks

and barbecue grills and ice box chests—

all bella bella chicas dressed in Tropical prints and rose

flower hair clips and flower brooches and spaghetti straps

and those brothers in rum reggae handmade Batik shirts

tomatoes grays and some in wife beater t-shirts showing distracting muscle

bulges boulder shoulders blasting biceps with Taino Tattoos of green

coqui tree frogs and Hibiscus Flower designs and wearing those bright

blue printed Flamingo Fedora hats across the Rockaway Beaches' parking lots

speaking in Spanglish, *yeah, jangear on the grassy areas*

where the beach balls and soccer balls are flying

and not on the sand and passing us as we going

home and I am smelling it's like a big block party barbecues

burning and they just beginning their beach day

when the suns going down because they already have a real dark tan

you always say that with your crooked-face smile.

at the cost of that weapon of surprise

RIP *Young Douglas Johnson 1954–1966*

They must have demolished the good old Marine Park Movie Theater, used to be right here, all dressed up in red velvet curtains, an aura of majesty demanding all its patrons be on their best behavior—People used to whisper and act all like they were in church. Uniformed ushers, ashtrays, double feature plus a cartoon. Yeah, Pink Panther. Bugs Bunny. Popeye the Sailor Man! *He's Popeye the Sailor Man/He's strong to the finish, cause he eats his spinach/ He's Popeye the Sailor Man!* It used to be right here. The redolent evocative smell of copper festering from a broken film tape flapping, film burning up or film break or scratch or they gotta change the reels of the spinning top rotating and wobbling as the projector wheel keeps herky-jerking raw and that reminds of-of that lingering metallic smell down avenue L and Nostrand as the small spindly body of a boy a school boy dragging on the back right wheel well of the bus slapping.

doodie on her swing

see my older brother Kenny and me walk down those alleyways barefooted on Brooklyn, New York's Parkville Avenue, to Judy's house to sit on her swing; we are four and five years old. we turn right down a hot city cemented side alleyway, like a buried secret lane where Coney Island Avenue in those borderlands where Kensington meets Ditmas Park meets Parkville, running behind shambling, double porched homes. hold your breath like when you are going through the Brooklyn Battery Tunnel in the family's station wagon cause those Callery pear trees, green crab apple trees smelling like a big stink up of rotting fish or of nanna's nasty feet-slipper smell, and the weeping cherry trees dangling, and drooping branches of glossy, dark green leaves with their blossoms atop like fallen white snow fountains captivating fragrances. each tree acting out like old men concierge of sorts in a phony- faux-class bouncer- police officers who lead the way to the hidden elbowmold smelling decrepit old-peoples' mildew-musty houses back there, and there on our right, is Judy's swing painted pink I go right into her backyard pretending to be carrying roasting sticks I carry on camping trips but are carrying broken branches with dog doodie on the tips, just looking like grub sticks like burnt-barbecued marshmallows on a homemade-skewer kit . . . and stinking up like dead stink-stank-stunk-skunks' stench and I wipe-*touch* that poop on her swing good. and yell out, "Judy, Judy gots doggiedoodie on her swing" run laughing-away, me pretending to be pigeon-toed on purpose and in a giggling-like stomach aching fit grab some cool-to-the-touch crabgrass bulbs inside of my toe-fingers and in fast motions in some somersaults, handstands, cart wheelings thinking we are getting so far away. laughing, laughing, laughing, spinning round and around like our plastic push and spin carousel spins. the sun moves up and down from the sky switching places with me and with the *the* old man concierge on one stiffened thigh like a twirling baton in the sky **hear** Judy's mom catapults out like a short stouted thunder bolt outta the back screen door, go-BANGBOP as that lady's arms akimbo and her eyebrow going up up and she fliPfloPsflipsfloPsfliPs flopping, flies me up like fake vomit hitting blue sky with a dirt-a-turd-crap-and-poo-ME up while my brother loping down the paved alleyway feet dip dip dip slaps smacking the hot cement, running longer and longer away like an avalanche

the relatives in Bay Ridge, Brooklyn

Aunt Evelyn had us over for her Sunday dinners out in Bay Ridge with mom and dad and she had thin striped ribbon candy bows and white with red stripes peppermint candy canes making me think of Saint Nickolas on the tip top the high mantel in a dish. *Don't eat all the candy,* mom said, *and be polite, say please and thank you. Bring a book and keep your mouths shut and don't fight. And Ken, don't drink too much of all of their beers,* my mommy always used to say. Then there was Rosemary who is my big cousin and there was her older sister too who had long pretty dirty-blonde hair and dressed like Nancy Campbell the nice girl across the street. And there was Johnny in high school is my cousin and always was studying inside his room off of the dining room and I would go to him and mess up his black slicked back hair. My Uncle Johnny Pinto called out names like New York Giants centerfielder Willie Mays, Jackie Robinson, the Dodgers, Gil Hodges, New York Yankees and the World Series standing in front of his brand new colored TV console deliriously happy and yelling out baseball jargon my daddy didn't know and hated to watch those sports shows always on the tv set there. And Uncle Pinto gave us collectable baseball cards with bubble gum inside. Our Uncle Johnny Canonico and Aunt Barbara living upstairs, the top floor, where I often went to baby sit the twins and young Johnny and my Grandpa Mike lived in the basement and I used to see his shaving cream brush right there in the tiny little sink past the pool table there. My Grandma Tessy still loved him and they both never got divorced cause we're Catholic and she stayed home alone when we all went on Sundays visiting the relatives out in Bay Ridge.

Where real important things are happening

Sattaday morning and sitting on a first stoop step wishing it was shaded by leaves, but it's the closest to the ground where real important things are happening

rather than somewhere else.

There's a rolly polly pill bug,

an armadillidiidae

is crawling out from the more moistest of all the spots and I'm wondering if it can float.

He sees a leggy ladybug then stops.

I aim a gust of air breath and curls inna ball. "*What do you wanna do?*" Cornelus and his sister Winnann always hasta always ask

and show off their vocab-alary and how they can count by fives.

I got on my brother's new pair of pink rubber soled sea cadet shoes on all polished a bright so white and his sailor hat folded in a tight cloth boomerang. I did take them from his room.

The kids are coming out soon,

I've already knocked on doors,

but Kathy Keenan can't come out till noon

and my brother is busy cracking heinie stick thermometers

and pulling them apart

and watching mercury spill

out into a pouring silver puddle on the ground. Then Brenda, Podrick and Miles Furlong

ask if we wanna make mud pie cakes behind their bloomed bigleaf hydrangeas'

puffy pink flower balls where no adults can see

and not even the bad kids who live across the street, but only the hunkering birds, and those black-capped chikadees celebrating their birds' nests in cavities can see

us playing in the bushes till our curfew is lightning bugs.

60s grammar school days

I sat at a wooden desk for years with folded hands with both feet on the floor.

Keeping still. Keeping quiet. Uniformed plaid and pleated and way passed the knees starched white shirt crisscrossed tie with woolen navy socks and the black Oxford shoes with Dad's spit shine shone.

I sat at a wooden desk for years. *How can I get good grades?* I would always ask myself.

If I sit straight and feet on floor and keep my bangs out of face and kept real short. If I don't talk and keep my desk tidy and clean I'm sure to get on honor roll.

Too afraid to give the wrong answers.

Too afraid to guess.

"See here. See here. Oh, that is just guess work you are doing," Sister Joseph Loretta would say.

"Oh," I would say.

Oh, irrevocable

There were drugs in the 60s in Brooklyn across the street from Navaare Pharmacy

where this big kid Mike Oburn lived inside that apartment was filled with the big high school kids that smoked pot and hashish, snorting heroin nickel bags, and some shooting up. Kip was a drug addict with swollen arms with needle holes and fat legs that could hardly walk. *He is a drug addict* the kids would say walking slowly like in a floating cloud down Avenue M. I said *hi Kip* acting like I am big because next year I will be an 8th grader and me wearing my Nehru paisley shirt and rushing back to the school yard to hang out in hope my teacher, Mr. Dorr, passes by me and I say *hi Mr. Dorr*, with my Hippi mandarin collar on, cool like when I had said *hi Kip* on my way down M and felt he was like the mayor of the avenue and that I could say hi to the slow walking monster. He said *go up to Mike's place; he's stopped breathing.* And I walked up the flight of stairs to see and there an ashen pallor or pale a grayish- blue a metalic skin the tall Mike spread out on the floor all so fart smelling stinky. My shoes stamped double sounds loud in a stairwell, echoing clip-clops clattering down the steps, with rapid shallow breathing breaths. I ran back down Avenue M without stopping and flew up the front foyer to my Grandma Tessy's always inside her kitchen in her house-dress apron on watching over the meatballs slowly fry simmering and says all lovingly *come sit with me.* And we both watch and listen to the same wet slap percolator coffee maker idling with me thinking about his breathless moments

the electrical shock

A white "Lady Kenmore" shaking a Hawaiian Hula and the electric white prahu drum tub

banging out a performance balancing too much inside and the oldest child with a yellow high and tight buzz cut, with dirty bugs bunny teeth, holding hands with sister, "Do you want to feel an electrical shock?" Sister's hand in hand with him and the little one. Three children under the wet clothes-pin line and me, miss tom boy pants, with one-cent-Double-Bubble-tattoo-arms, whose ten in a three-handed-red-tight-fisted band of holdin hands in bare foot percussions smacking themselves in puddles wet. His finger, pointing to the hula jerking hard and announcing "*Ready. Set. One. Two. Three,*" and touches the metal machine and an electrical current gets through the three. The littlest one, chubby white and small, and wearing a tattered-daggy-dress-with-dangy-dirty-arms, yelps out a stifled scream, flown bang-against-the-wall like wet clay.

that Staten Island ferry ride in the early 60s

They built the Verrazano Narrows Bridge for us to visit Uncle Jack & Aunt Mickey and our cousins on 62 Suffolk Avenue in Castleton Corners, to the Southernmost borough. The orange ferry tugging through the ragged yellow and green waters but far from the deepest spot of blue out there closer to the Statue always with a crowd of tourists on deck taking photos as it passes her standing proudly wearing the color of 30 million pennies a brownish greenish with her

     torch burning looking through binoculars hoping to see some whales but spotted foot-propelled diving birds feeding on the bobbing rocking-horse a carcass of a giraffe blown up along the interface with its long heavy neck bowing between the water and the breezy wind-driven back

and forth with outsized clown eyes expressing sorrowful emotions a slapping long tongue loose and floating the collapsing of the giraffe the SPECTACULAR circus ferry's first live action thriller runs off into the Hudson River and the people take pictures of the Brooklyn Bridge and Empire State Building the Chrysler Building and lower Manhattan from the boat and look never look back far out. And I'm asking which is taller the Empire State Building or Statue of Liberty but am getting so hungry smelling grilled hot dogs they're selling pretzels inside the snack bar but daddy says he's got an insulated bag of hot dogs in his car and a cooler of sodas and beers.

but daddy can't read

To my dad who was not a reader or a writer—love you daddy

the blowing-of-a-nose sound comes in through the open-dining-room window

from the-upstairs-kitchen window of the duplex, right next door,

woo-ish woo-ish honk

The sheer curtains puff the summer's air, just a bit and in comes that

woo-ish woo-ish honk

the blowing-of-a-nose noise. "Oh, that's Dottie Herrmann's nose din from next door," my daddy tells me and then laughs with cigarette smoke coming out his ears.

"Hi, Dottie, hellooooo," Kenny Cunningham whispers to himself aloud to allow me to hear. Lifts two finger gestures out a wave.

La de da, Dot. Hallo.

" *Guten Morgen!*"

"*Guten Tag*"

 What's the craic?

Ahoy-hoy hoi

Woo-ish woo-ish honk

"That's Dottie playing that double reed like two reeds on a contrabassoon. **You** laughing **didn't** laughing laughinglaughinglaughinglaughing hahahahehehe **know** laughing **she could play?**"

Then daddy doodles on a napkin with a pen

With how quickly he-

cursives-his-first-and-last-names-a-memorized-sight-word-he-knows

with one barreling movement amagicianunderpressureasIlook.

"Oh, Dot, yes. She goes long way back. Me and Dot went to different high schools together."

"Oh, Daddy," I say.

discovering patterns and poetry

My daddy, Kenny Cunningham, drove a canary-colored cab. Working a five-borough night while I lay across the front seat with a pillow and a sheet looking in the back at the strangers, in wet raincoats. Peek-a-booing between the tight space between the two front seats. Faces disappear then reappear, disappear, reappear looking back at them while jingling coins inside my daddy's metal changer, methodically. And now they are smiling again like they appeared again before. The money meter's clicking like our dining room cuckoo cuckoo clock ticking but the melodious canary doesn't cuckoo *or* even come outta tha door of the clock anymore. That lady's hand is a up and down mashing a glowing cigarette in the dark circles around to the portable stainless-steel stinken cigar car round push down ashtray with a spinning tray like Aunt Paula's banging the pink Spalding ball, inside of an old knee-high sock, tied into a knot, on the top, the back and forth, in the alley way, against the wall, singing "Mary Mack. Miss Mary/Mack Mack Mack all dressed in/ black black black with silver/ then the shuffling of wet boots squeaking on the floor. The wind shield wipers *swinging* back and forth like resonating Oh *hail the taxi man   Oh, hail the taxi man* rain patters against the window an wipers changing their verse to clack-thrum, clack-thrum. then to patter pitter pa tar pit tar pa tar pit tar like paternosters said volubly in a car driving inside a rain shower. My right hand is tapping

whaurrthesepatternscomesfrom? Whaurrthesepatternscomesfrom? like the repetition of hand clappen patty cake, patty cake, and Rockin Robin's "Every little swallow, every chick-adee" with lots of kids' hands clappen. the changer's rattling rack while I'm thinking I wanna learn how the black girls synchronize, an inward jump to two long ropes in Double Dutch. Singing Bluebells, cockle shells, / Eevie, ivy, over; an I am thinking. Then there's pictures but not sound patterns on Aunt Judy's Catskill Mountains trucker hat snapback high peaks hiking wall paper with rack pack racoons and cats in cars and a Niagara Falls oval-motion lamp spinning like a whirly wheel top toy on the floor plugged in. And my Brooklyn Grandma Tessy's Christmas mugs with written down musical notes on lines. The lyrics to a lithograph of a brush on the snow, when my daddy's "Oh, my De De Diddly Dee, Dee Diddles Dee " singing out my names to me driving.

my Lancelot

When Times Square was sleazy 1980s

the shadiest block in America with sex market drug trade

homeless encampments pock marked and dotted its streets

the peep shows the porn movies the prostitutes standing there

and me handing out advertisement papers

a human billboarded ad walker

 wearing a six feet four inches tall, President Abe Lincoln Hat

a newly hired promotional sandwich walking billboard

a Barbizon model getting her first job that Open Call, castings on a go-see for a modeling booking

wearing form fitting shirt and blue skinny jeans

and I called you on the public phone

crying.

You leaned out your mighty checkered taxi cab and shut off its engine in the middle of 42

and you saw me and I saw you

my shining knight with all the codes of chivalry

all the qualities of bravery, courtesy, all with great gallantry

not on a horse but in a yellow taxi

my daddy

You threw that outfit flying across 42nd street

went flying over the dirty horrible bad city street

like how you toss your home-made pizza dough like a true pizzaiolo. My hero

 asking what my favorite Drakes Cake was

and that made my crying into loud laughter

seeing all of those delicious Yodels Devil Dogs

Funny Bones Ring Dings and the coffee cakes on the backjump seat

too hot to sleep

Sometimes the curtains were the only beautiful thing about a fan in the window at night with thoughts of a shade tree and a hose with my nose against the metal mesh screen saying Our Father and Hail Mary's with my head resting on the pane and certainly God was breathing me to sleep in the graceful movements of cool breeze through the open windows and sites of gibbous designs in the night time sky. The fireflies, like waning moons and stars making me wish I were Peter Pan in fairy dust, flies far away, and then that single breeze along with the crickets making stridulating sounds, mosquitoes' buzz buzz and the flies' hum when evening changes night into crinkled sheets, window fans, and screens.

the beehive hairdo

My Aunt Paula wanted to play with my hair cause she said it was stringy knots. She yelled out grandma's window to come upstairs for a new hairdo. I went up the front stoop steps and up the foyer stairs. She asked if I wanted the Beehive, Flipped Bob or Mop Top Beetles cut but mommy said no cutting. She twisted a pony on top of my head and bobby pinned it down and she said she needed to *tease my tail with a comb and spray* stinky sticky stuff. My mommy, Aunt Marylou and Grandma were clapping, and all were so happy so proud. But I sat and said I wanted to take it this all puffy all out. Then she wanted to put pink lip stick and eye lines under my eyes and I ran down the twisting back steps through the dark room and passed the burp spitting furnace and up the steps to my house where my daddy always was. He looked at my hair and dried my tears and washed my hair right out and took me for a walk—we both bouncing our pink spalding rubber balls down to get a vanilla malted at Bennies candy store on M.

but my mommy says

Johnny DeJohn's brother Tony D. is calling out his girlfriend Vickie's name real loud in the streets and wears a cigarette pack rolled up in his T-shirtsleeve a bad boy yelling hysterically shouting combing his Brylcreemed D.A. duck's ass slicked-back with a wide- tooth comb crying and Peggy and Richard are in the alleyway smoochugging and I'm thinking when I get big kissing will probably just go out of style but paisley prints and bell-bottoms are too expensive for my mom to buy at Macy's but she knows how to make pink tie-dyes in the sink and the clothes with psychedelic prints with neon colors grandma never sews for me and mommy doesn't like when I mismatch patterns and break up my top and shorts' matching sets that are supposed to be worn together. My mommy says to look at Nancy Campbell who lives across the street who wears mod styles but with pastels to look like our fashionable First Lady in the White House to look like a nice girl like a nurse who is so compassionate, kind and polite and no miniskirts that the hemline should fall two inches below the knee and not ever higher. But Diane Fogarty who lives down the block near M says the F word out loud and tugs her school uniform skirt up from the waist and her thighs are showing on purpose, I think. I think about the girl who lives across the street who got thrown from a building in Greenwich Village from the leader of the Hell's Angels motorcycle club gang and died dead in 1977 in the street and her mom gave my mom all of her expensive clothes like the filmy Juliet Capulet's would wear with enormous long-sleeve lace up or a ruffled Renaissance in velvet dresses in rich fabric and accented with sparkly jewels, gold cords and all stuffed into bags just for me.

At least I know where she is now, she told my mommy.

It's daddy's nighttime

My daddy worked for Borders Milk Company with Uncle Anthony who spoke broken English mixed with Italian from New Jersey when he couldn't find a job and that is where that big garbage can filled with Hershey's Cocoa Unsweetened chocolate powder to make chocolate milk is in his workshop under the shelves on the floor comes from Uncle Anthony. He had to be on the truck at 3:00 in the morning from the Bronx where it wasn't a safe spot to go and said he saw a man frozen dead some where I forget now but that's when I started tying on a string to the front door through the living room through the dining room down the hallway and up my bunk bed and around my wrist. When daddy came home the string would pull and I would think *aww daddy's home.* And then you would hear him snap open a beer because he says it's his nighttime and it's only our morning. He would polish and spit shine our school shoes and line the up along the wall and make pancakes and cook up the bacon and eggs splattering sounds in the frying pan. He put the white bread on the flame and made Irish Toast that tastes like burned bread a bit but always tasted good.

Myrtle the box turtle

I miss the McKiernan's box turtle called Myrtle in their yard just four doors down towards L. They feed him bits of chop meat and mealworms a few times in a week. Then leafy greens like kale, collards and mustard greens he'll eat, and my sister and Terry rip off Nanna Herrmann's hyacinth and duckweed and Kathy sneaks some lettuce from her fridge. I asked my grandma for some cucumbers and beets and she said give that turtle some crickets, flies and spiders you can find and leave the fridge door shut. Myrtle would lumber agreeably towards us then stop and continue across the patio path and stretch his long reptilian neck and look side to side then stop again looking back. Then disappearing in a pile of pine needle duff. Then we all ran down to L to feed Shamus the Pekin duck in that fenced in yard was a special friend of mine. She was white and quacking and sometimes on a leash with a great long enthusiastic noisy beak quacks quack and had a big plastic pool filled with water to its brim and splashes and orange nose drinks with flapping wings and runs to the gate to get a piece of lettuce from my hand. But I have a pet rabbit a companion in my home cause my daddy found it in the road on Easter Sunday morning two years back and he hops around my living room my albino Florida, red- eyed-white with lots of stretches and hop hops and eats freshly bought hay from Grandpa's house in Saugerties and daddy says rabbits are not low-maintenance at all and wonders if Grandpa wants to cook him in Uncle Tom and Aunt Joan Vaclaversacks' big old kitchen soup pot.

remembering that dead art of tv repair

Mr. McKiernan, a neighbor four doors down, came right to our home to fix anything small appliances, electronics and especially tv repairs because carrying heavy consoles was impractical. He played with those metal rabbit ears or the rotary clicker thing on its base the antenna to get the best picture set. He used to come to our house with a mirror on a tripod to see what the picture was doing when he was changing vacuum tubes and making adjustments from behind sometimes he turned off the set making daddy hunt for his cigarettes hoping to watch Hogan's Heroes and football is on tonight. And Mr. McKiernan would say if you only lived in Elmhurst like his cousin's building gets that direct line of sight to the King of all buildings the chosen master antenna site that Empire State but here, we get treetops and popular leaves and I get those mud daubers, spiders and lizards in my sets in the New Jersey summer home so consider yourself a lucky man here on New York Avenue when there is no flying irascible lightning bolts followed by that crack sound of thunder and that'll kill ya dead.

 And there, in early August I walked behind that lot across Bohack's supermarket on Nostrand with overgrown giant weeds and rag weeds was once this old Motorola tv abandoned with cut wires and unscrewed screws from that circuit board bright green in the grass broken apart left to rot and rust with the arsenic, cadmium, chromium and barium spilling out and someone broke the picture tube glass and I'm the tv repair fix it man among the swaying nettles and the butterflies and bumblebees and me playing with the silvery watery, the mercury and crumbling up layers of the cinnamon-brown mica like crystalline sparkles crumbling

From Flatbush, with love

I come from a city where one is not enough, made do and fell between two, and found love. The song and poem sung by one whose heart and soul make up the strength of all omnipotent winds is Mohammad-Deeb-Hashim- Saleh-Elkheir, my Muslim Lebanese. He's a pretty man with haunted eyes, one blue and one darkened green. Then there is the sea a symbol of my love Shapoor Ghiahi, a naval officer, who is far away.

My love between the wind and sea, a hard tune and melody. How can love be in harmony and shy between the two? Wetting-my-foot-upon his bow while wind blow and blow.

Years too full of misery meaning mourns a minstrelsy. And visiting my sailorman in port cities in Iran: Bandar Abbas, Bandar-e Anzali, Bandar-e- Emam Khomeyni, Bandar-e Lengeh

Bandar-e Mahshahr, and in fear of the angry crowds hid inside of a black,

floor-length chador, searching for my love Shapoor,

Shapoor Giahi. How hot the southern coast of Iran was, on the narrow-Strait-of- Hormuz. The presence of my love, my sailorman, weakened me as he stood, a

uniformed seafarer in white, tall, dark and Persian

The winds cooled my face as he was blown some distance away

and-with-one-foot-on-deck and-one-on-shore,

the winds tossing sailors and seagulls like shards of white paper in the wind. The wind on the brig breathes -and-blows drowning my sailor in my dreams and only hoping that he can swim.

His warship lies there at anchor waiting dormant, immovable, and me waiting for the wind and ocean to fall upon me dreaming of a tidal wave that wet me all over, covered with wet white, forced, cut up red, by the roughness of sand and shell, soothe my longing me.

Thrown on shore as crippled things and dead things are thrown to shore.

Watching waves caress itself as it pulls out backward to the sea,

Coming back again coming again wetting me. No, let me remember what my dream was really like: Sun-burnt belly, fleshy raw on the breathing seashore. Oh, the Ocean's got-a-real-salty tongue feathery- felt-forked- Fingers-and thumb wipes me down and swallows me.

The wind and ocean have broken my heart, leaving me breathless and pale.

 Creating me into a desert, loose and drifting. Suffocating the wind to its last ghastly breath.

My blowing sands will not pile into dunes or sand hills but fill the depth of the sea

leaving it dry as it leaves me. My sand will swirl among the Arab, lost and wandering. Oh, with their blackened brown eyes, with their voices singing harshly under the toils of the sun and of the moon, they pass over me gently. Making their one brow rise, as my sand will play upon their features wisping through and surrounded with hair of black blue glistering. Stealing their kisses,

 as they brush my sands from their mouths. Filling ears with sighs, teasing their eyes

tangling their minds with vagaries of mirages of- sands - of- winds-of -seas they'll pass over me gently. Passions that will never meet again or know.

M e

everlastingly dre a m i n g.

An Irish Gavotte Dance to the Catskills from Flatbush

Sullivan-doubled house in Saugerties go around and round an Adirondack-rocker-chaired porch like a lovely Up State New York luxury resort. Once you go inside the front door, there is a curving banister that works itself down a 2-story entry foyer with large bare walls. We are coming three hours from Flatbush, Brooklyn to Grandpa's in the mountains, with running water creeks, with stepping-stone stairs, outta stuck slate slabs, and stones. And my Grandpa always says to keep an eye out for those swimming snakes that look like black, wooden poles and those cunning leprechauns hiding their pots of gold! If you are looking at the staircase as you enter through the front door, Aunt Judy's side of the house is to the left and always the town's friendly dog sprawls out on the floor and we ballet around and round him, but he won't never bite.

The crooked, bent floored all things tilting into a high hill kitchen is in the back of the parlor. I remember Aunt Judy saying, "Don't put your bottles of bubbles or glasses or cups or saucers down on this kitchen table cause they'll all spill and fall on the floor. And don't drink the sink water it smells like rust and rotten eggs." Then there is this white wooden door that leads to a lingering hallway upstairs, smelling like old-people's elbows. If you can shuffle dance the basic steps up those white painted stairwell steps, you'll get to a lingering hall, where you can pass by opened bedroom doors and strangers will be sitting on white enamel painted brass beds, cause Grandpa painted everything white that year. We peek in each door and see someone sitting on the bed or in a chair or just standing there and we shake out our hands limp and pirouette changing from heel first walking to toes first walking from a parallel placed step to a turned-out rhythmic way down the hallway and giggling.

Then in the big room to the right of the upstairs banister is Nana dying in her bed. I say, so hush-hush, she's sleeping. But while your demi-plie is in position by the door you can hear her breathing. Do a thraneen or a bit more of practice of pointing feet, and a stretch one two release. Then tip toe up to the vestibule window next to Nana's room on one foot or two feet, you'll see fireflies glowing so gracefully in falling sweeps. If you listen, you can hear night crickets' white noise and cicada wings' teeth chattering like it's a passing diesel train noisy. Can you hear them prattling their symphony of da da da da di di di da da da da.

Coast down the banister but once never. Come on put your socks on so our feet can't be stoppers and hide your hands inside of some old shirt sleeves and stomach glissade down and your chin hits the front door and sometimes knocks unconscious in the fall. Look to the right is Aunt Judy's door and then look to the left, is the gas burning heater, the lazy boy chair, and can you hear the Irish step dancing music sounding dancers with stiffened arms straight tight sided wearing hard-heavy worn foot nailing floorboards tight precise movements of feet flaming motions moving See that's my Grandpa and Grandma Gee Bee's door. Look to your right and you see Aunt Judy's living room and that dog's still there. And once you visit Grandpa, you'll see him sitting in his chair, remember to pass him belly creeping cross the floor, so he can't get you, but he wud, in his arms, and then you're stuck there for some time spent. Grandma Gee Bee would be embroidering curved triangles into bluebells and roses on linen inside of where all new plumb-leveled floored kitchen is but she's up and down jigging right there near the fridge, where the iced cold red Kool Aid is and is sounding whimsically-Dingle-or-Cork but not at all from Tipperary, whose foot slip jiggins doubling time, gets more louder, a roaring, a frozen electric, a gravity freezing the switching, the stomping in her hard-soled-shoes.

The Woodstock Campers behind My Grandpa's the Sullivan House

For the three days of the festival in Bethel, in Sullivan County, and on its south east shore of Ulster landing Park is Saugerties where I was on vacation the same time Woodstock 1969 was held on a dairy farm in the Catskill Mountains, between Aug 15-19 and Jimi played on Monday at 9:00 a.m., the Star-Spangled Banner immortalized on film but I never heard about Woodstock or of any of the bands playing then—I was a young 14 year old who was really like a much younger than a ten.

There were lots of camping guests sleeping in Grandpa's creek and their floating white bars of ivory soap and nudity—in his waterfalls and I was watching them from the barn behind daddy's target practice stakes and plates. They had pitched up tents with campfires in the dark.

Then early morning when my daddy wanted to go fishing for Rainbow Trout, Chain Pickerel, and Bass, so we were pulling out the Night Crawlers and Red Wigglers from Grandpa's worm pit, a big part of the slope, in his yard, behind and right past his shed and barn. We both saw them sitting where my chalk sticks and pictures tagged *this is my flat rock to sit upon.*

They drew lots of pastel pink Peace signs, Yin and Yang and drew some broken hearts

and released my bottled bubbles with my wand.

And my daddy said they're the smoken skunk on top of furred hawk-weeds, the purple needlegrass, the dropseed and the panicled foxtail and stones, and right under the snowy feathery Fringe'-trees, my father's favorite shrubs. We traipse to daddy's secret place to fish, through those long short cuts through more woods and country roads all its smelling like my tadpole tank hidden in my grandpa's shed mixed with scent of the fragrances of green leaves, rose flowers and a floral scent reminiscent of a potted perfumery geranium rose and hear my daddy whispering *aw this is our own cheap* escape *like each being on our own run-away carousal horse our natural escape when we wander back behind your grandpa's home in the Catskill Mountains.*

The banging of pots, pot covers, metal spoons on pans

Saying goodbye to Grandpa John, Grandma-GB and Aunt Judy was more than just an obstructive choke in the throat. It was more than just holding back the tears. It was the not knowing when we will be able to get back like always maybe next summer. And now I see it was not the three-hour ride that was the difficult part; it was the finding a car that worked for three hours straight there to Saugerties, and back to Brooklyn and it was Dad being able to get the vacation days off all in a row.

There, the three stood, in the road with their hidden instruments behind their backs.   We all packed in the station wagon with the suitcases and the pillows and the spreading out bedsheets in the back and in the road where Grandpa in his pajamas and Grandma's

beginning to bang pot covers on kitchen pots and Aunty Jewels holding the pan with a metal spoon behind her back looking like proud drummers dressed in cotton robes and slippers they stood out in the middle of the country road belt-bash-biff-blow bopping until we couldn't see them anymore belt-bash-biff-blow bopping until we couldn't hear them anymore and that lump knobby in the throat lasted till we were far passed old Elden's gas station and heard mom and dad's flying wind-muted talkings about Elden's last senile moments outside without any clothes or shoes on like how the winter trees etched, displaying limbs stripped naked, clean and sharp against the frozen landscape. Elden found the unfurling of that hoary winter's snow-covered roads with temperatures of zero and below and the chilling wind sighing through the grip.

my father's face

I saw him toothless and pink gummed

with lips

quietly

straining his exhausted face

slowly fuses

into the hospital bed

morphined

his hand holding a ghost cigarette

every now and then he takes

a drag.

He lifts open his eye lids

and gives me his usual loving smile

that Kenny Cunningham smile

that bartender's grin

that yellow-cabby-bright face.

Then he relaxes back into his pillow like melted vanilla ice cream.

from a lighted meteoroid shooting around in outer space

Too heavy a mound

               now falling

down in through the Earth and uninterruptedly out through the

Brahmaputra and back up into space.

               Hello? Can you hear me?

I can't throw out the little piles of memorabilia of your childhood. There are things deposited on top of me, one layer at a time, sheet by sheet, mounding like an artificial Falls Church City, Virginia-Mohenjo-Daro, bit by bit, year by year, falling matter, little by little, and by those that heralded before me, too heavy a mound, your books, your poems, your short stories, your photographs, your paintings, your type writer collection beginning with the Lillian Rose 1945 and Vanessa Greene, Hemmingway's kind and the Daisywheel and the white Smith Corona, the 'locket,' gold plated, inscribed with a fancy 1900's fancy cursive F font (Nuno's dad: Francesco), there's Nuno's collection of old guitar strings, "used, but 'like new' he labelled them, there's the Baron's things like Amide's portrait of his grandma, 1898, who lived thru Civil War, maybe gold rush period, there's Memere's mom's pancake mixing bowl and favorite spatula and Great Grandma Tessy's china closet and buffet from the early 50s here at home with me, there's grandma's wedding ring, it's old and went through 60 years of marriage with Grandpa Kenny, just for you to take, there's an assortment of things, calling out while sitting crisscross applesauce position under my make-shift bed-blanket-and-bed-sheet tent, like a kid at night with a flash light emitting some brightness floating on the circumambient air from the "days in the past, covered up little by little, those that preceded them and are themselves buried beneath those that follow them . . . " (Proust). Only when I am well away past sleeping, safely nestled into my favorite sleeping position inside of my collapsible shelter inside of my falling warmonger house from a Lighted Meteoroid Shooting Around in Outer Space—when a thought of falling far out, just me, into space, in orbital float position, it's no longer a problem had—only inside these swirls of childhood's newness to darkness' strange shapes of various bursts of colors, spilling its contents brutally apart and what a pleasure as I have no right to but

release

all the materialistic

into space,

because children are our arrows and they fly far through without being burdened down with all of that junk stuff—only in my newness of living an unexpected liberty has arisen (in which thinking of dwindling into eternity— is really fun) do I intuit the real reasons for

my newly ecstatic barrage, vacating selves

to the sinuous shapes,

eye floating clumpy or stringy dots,

of light and dark,

these miraculous

curvilinear bright swirl-rhythms.

a heavy upon the world

Around inside my mind I came out here in my gazebo to write a sonnet but can find no other words than I feel so sad tonight. I volunteered and helped Emma and 96-year-old George.   I think that's his name, but it could be Charles.

I feel so sad, even though I did my chores and gardening. I feel so sad. The night-bug symphony has long ago started with the bug chirps and chippering'-s, but I can't smile.

The maids came and cleaned my home and I brought fresh flowers.

My son will visit me soon and still I can't smile. I pour a glass of Chianti and sip in the darkness in my garden, but I feel so sad tonight for that wet fish felon in the weeds: silent, with silver fins getting muddy in the cool dry earth in the darkness.
Suffocating. What does he have to do to get his career life back again? He served his time there, four years long___ And when will he get his chance to improve his reputation? What does it mean to serve your time? What does it mean to forgive? Where is his redemption ticket? I am somewhere in the mud digging with him, distressed as he tries to cleanse past misdeeds, searching, pushing away from righteous judgments wanting to head straight towards the sun. Can't a phoenix resurrect? Can't you hear it clawing?

anthropomorphizing

My Dearest Microbial Yeast Organisms:

You do read this letter as though it is a friendly letter, but do you notice the colon there? Despite this important uncertainty of how you actually take how-this-letter-is-written is not up to you this time. You talk to me only when you want, and our relationship is rather long and ambiguous since I was five on Parkville Avenue sitting there in front of Saint Rose a Lima Church in 1962. I sat by the stone statues talking to you.

And here you always are talking techniques of kneading, of shaping of pounding poetic protuberances into the Villanelle and the Virelay.

Oh, my microscopic fungus. my mushrooms my mold my

reproducing buddlets blows. I'm hurt by you.

Oh, you say you see a white bit of paper in the wind

getting blown into the spreading lily

and you give me butterflies drinking nectar from flowers through their tongues

just sounding like squarking inhalations of seagulls in the air bending the throttle

the boats I mean

tied docked

anchored there

chained seagulls in the night's air

How would these words look like scattered, if not on paper is all I am asking to be told? Can I capture each impression and glue it on the page or tie each meaning to a post to rescue you from abstraction? or will a camera over power the way of verbal stress so I can outdo, vividness? Your gestures I'll keep a secret if I to fall in love, your meaning I would not dare describe if if you let me see. I'll recite I'll recite your poetry not to bade goodbye, not to change a line. Can I be your imagery? I'll be your special tone. Will you share your breath with me and tell me what's not been told?

don't leave me here alone without you. And I know the fishermen do dream but not of taxes, prices or profits from their catch

and me too. My Dearest Microbial Yeast Organisms, I love you.

An ode to Trader Joe's Flowers

In Memory of Aunt Mary Lou and Aunt Gloria

And now I too can afford some fresh flowers to put on my table at home where the woody scents and colors of the Ranunculus and Tulips all dressed in baby breath and greenery bring the relaxed atmosphere and mood of my day just like how it was as a young child seeing my Aunt Mary Lou and Aunt Gloria. Oh, how wonderful their smiles were right there like the soft sweet smelling rose bouquets and bags of the five almond party favors always left over from the Italian wedding parties. And if they showed up at my punch ballgame, I would hit-fist the pink Spalding ball high and far at least two sewers down the street bringing me super power strength from these two sidewalk flowers in silent bloom found there flowering out of the concrete-pavement-cement standing there but now right here on my table with me bought from Trader Joe's are both of you are still right here with me in floral fragrance

scrap paper on Ars Poetica

Shhhhhhh, while whispering in a quiet small voice in the inner portion of tha hall. It's eight minutes passed midnight but time doesn't matter cause the nosey sill still near enough can hear. Poetry is anthro po morph ism spreading itself all over the place and more or like fast growing vines of the grabbing Wisteria disguises as tree monsters who shimmy on stiffened thighs providing thick canopies among the bombilating cicada with chilly chattering teeth on wings mouthing out *"da da da da da da-dadada. it's tooooooo cold. it's too cold da-da-da- da*

-da-da-da-da. Helpa-pa-pa-pa me we are dying. It's unfriendly freezing out here."

and now how hopeless we all feel.and there on tha floor my stuffed owl toy hoots, *"it should be snowing now,"* he hoots more *"snowing so sooooooon but not yet."*

And we hear all this on purpose from the window in the hall cause like us and some smaller too, listen and see all these entities and what they do and the inanimates, they do-so-talk they-so-do and along with those prattling -florid-flamboyant-flamingoes passing in-the-sky, flying flying by, where knees bend in backwards separate in segments folds in fifths in flight while they are, right now, looking back. Can ya see? Look away

and don't forget to birdcage them all inside a writing pad then pretend we are pigeon toed on purpose, and walk around like becoming expressive through our footwork, through our fancy footwork through our two left almost touching thumb tope-sharks

over lapping so they won't see we see they don't want to be captured in our poetry

or in a shower of spark-sized those fly away phosphenes. They don't want to be personified or to be epitomized as worn out cliché that can never withstand the pillars of e tern i t y

and like freed felons, they walk again smelling the vellichor, swirling, curling in the ripe dewy petrichor of our abandoned years ago, a hidden annex of our childhood.

Ode to the Ginkgo Biloba tree and to her leaves

Now it comes to me that you fan-shaped leaves right in front of the Hermann's house, in Brooklyn on New York Avenue next door to my old house cause we had a parking sign pole instead of a tree and there were those leaves now I know were from a Gingko Biloba tree—fell yellow. I didn't know your name then or why your golden fall lobed leaves, like tiny Japanese paper fans, fell differently than the Giordano's maple tree. Now feeling the fresh fall air just reminiscing about you. You are not like the maple, the sycamore, or the sweetgum tree. Thinking of always seeing you in yellow fall on the avenue with your parted cleavage scattering in sheer fall camisoles with one missed blouse button and though you are classy, you are from a street tree, a living fossil 350 million years old making you the oldest tree on earth from the era of dinosaurs. You are the earliest of my leaf-time memories of not thinking you were really a leaf. You Ms.—silver apricot—maidenhair tree, every leaf brings me right back to you.

my mom moves in with me after when dad passes

All Brooklyn moved to Florida and you and dad did too. You an Italian American woman who was married over sixty years to Kenny and wanted to die when he passed away, but you came to live with me and the boys in Falls Church City, Virginia and I've been a long time away from your home.

You come with your suitcase and your grandchildren and my homestay International students from all over the world greet you at my wide-open door while you come in tripping over Saudi students bowing down in prayer on the living room floor. And the seven years passed by so quickly and you were so lovely mom as I ever your carefree smile sparkled seeing you laughing with the Russian, with that funny tall Turkish student, Oscar, who always talked about himself. You with the African, the Japanese with the Muslims, with the Protestant Christians too, with the Black American and Latinos, You letting go of that white fragilities, that good/bad binary, opening yourself up to not excluding or marginalizing remembering negative racial stereotyping and those growing up Brooklyn days and then awakening and the panic attacks slowly found solace in understanding love. God had a plan.

Then one evening you say you see a big beautiful table over there inside of that room.

"Oh, you never showed me that big beautiful table or that room. How lovely that table is dressed in bowls of fruit and drink and flowers in vases over there. Can you see? Can you take me there?"

And you walk into your bedroom to get your walker, your pocketbook and knitting supplies and wool.

Oh, mom, where are you going? Come rest on your bed in your room.

I found you in the morning in the same position I left you that night. You passed so quickly from this life. No hospitals, no nurses, no surgery. You passed so quickly from this life. Jesus took you to his father's house where there are many rooms. He took you that night.

www.ingramcontent.com/pod-product-compliance
Lightning Source LLC
Chambersburg PA
CBHW072016060426
42446CB00043B/2565